Lila and Andy learn about

Biomimicry

Discover Amazing Designs Borrowed from Nature

Kenneth Adams

Book Cover by Kenneth Adams
Illustrations and Images by Kenneth Adams
Illustrations and Images created with AI assistance
First Edition 2025

ISBN: 978-1-998552-22-1

Your ideas can change the world!

This book belongs to:

_____

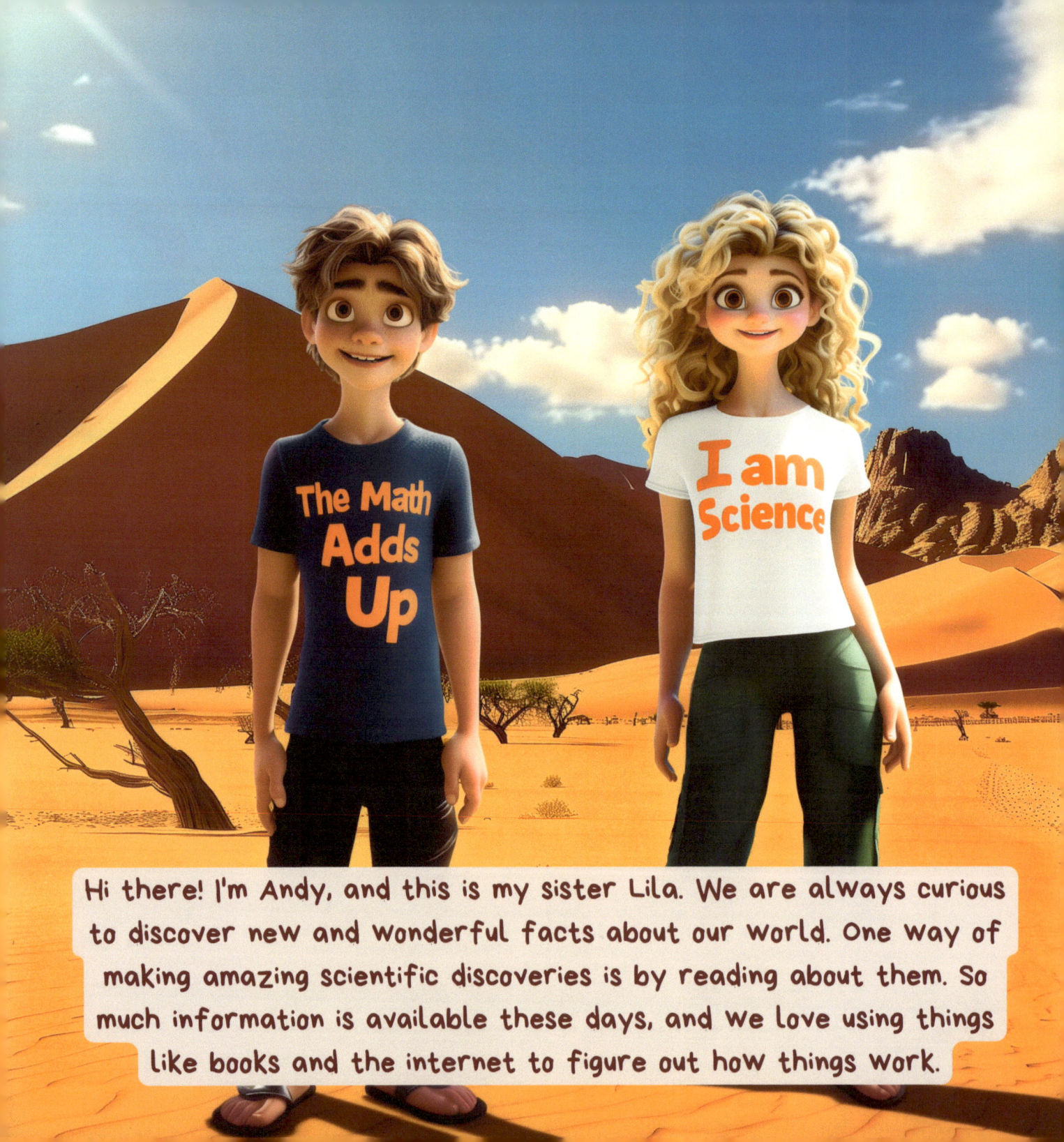

The Math
Adds
Up

I am
Science

Hi there! I'm Andy, and this is my sister Lila. We are always curious to discover new and wonderful facts about our world. One way of making amazing scientific discoveries is by reading about them. So much information is available these days, and we love using things like books and the internet to figure out how things work.

We recently visited Namibia, an African country that is home to the world's oldest desert, the Namib Desert. Scientists believe this desert is more than 55 million years old. That's a long time to be a desert! One day, while playing on a sand dune, we noticed tiny lizards called geckos running around on the hot sand. They are the cutest little animals and can survive in harsh climates like the desert.

We also saw them running up and down the windows and walls of the hotel we were staying in, and that made us wonder how they can stick to the walls and glass so easily. That's when Dad, who happens to be an engineer, told us about something called biomimicry.

He explained that scientists have been studying how these tiny lizards stick to objects, and all their research inspired the invention of many different types of tapes and glues that we use to stick things together! We were amazed to learn that scientists and engineers study nature all the time to solve human problems and create incredible new technologies.

Today, we're super excited to share what we've learned about biomimicry, the amazing science of copying nature's best ideas to make our lives better. Get ready to discover how everything from burr seeds to shark skin has inspired inventions that might be in your own home right now!

What is Biomimicry?

Biomimicry is like being an excellent detective in nature, discovering all the awesome things animals can do, and then using that science to invent stuff that helps us as humans! The word is made up of two parts. "Bio" means life, and "mimicry" means to copy or imitate. So biomimicry means to copy life!

Plants and animals have developed incredible ways to survive in nature. Over millions of years, they've figured out how to stick to walls, fly efficiently, stay waterproof, and thrive in harsh environments. Engineers and scientists study these exceptional natural solutions and ask, "How can we use these incredible ideas to help people?"

Think about it this way: Nature's designs are incredibly well-developed. A bird's wing, a spider's web, or a gecko's toe pad work amazingly well to help each animal survive in its specific habitat. Nature has figured out these amazing solutions that are incredibly efficient and effective.

Did you know?
Polar bear fur isn't actually white. It's transparent and hollow like tiny straws, which traps warm air so efficiently that scientists copied it to create better insulation for buildings!

Did you know?
A woodpecker's beak hits trees 20 times per second without getting a headache, which inspired engineers to design better football helmets and shock-absorbing materials for cars!

When we practice biomimicry, we try to understand why something in nature works so well and then figure out how to use that principle to solve human challenges. Sometimes, the solution we come up with looks exactly like the way it appears in nature, and sometimes, it looks completely different but uses the same scientific principle.

The coolest part? Biomimicry often helps us create inventions that are better for the environment. After all, nature doesn't create waste; everything has a purpose and fits together perfectly in the ecosystem.

The Things We Learn From Nature

The Namib Desert Beetle and Fog Harvesting

In the Namib Desert, where it seldom rains, lives a small beetle with an amazing ability to find water!

This clever little beetle spends its days crawling over burning hot sand under the blazing sun, but it never gets thirsty. How does it do this? The secret is on its back! Thousands of tiny bumps, smaller than the width of the hair on your head, cover the beetle's shell.

When morning fog drifts in from the nearby ocean, water droplets stick to these tiny bumps. As more and more water collects, the droplets grow bigger and heavier. Then gravity pulls them down special channels on the beetle's shell, sending fresh water flowing right into its mouth! It's like having your own personal water delivery system.

Scientists studying this amazing beetle had a brilliant idea. They built large nets that copy the beetle's bumpy shell design. When fog rolls through these nets, water droplets stick to them, grow bigger, and drip into collection containers below.

Today, people collect thousands of gallons of fresh water from thin air in places where they once struggled to find even a single drop. From the mountains of Peru to the coasts of Morocco, these beetle-inspired water collectors are turning morning mist into life-changing resources. Sometimes the smallest creatures hold the keys to solving our biggest problems!

Gecko Feet and Super Adhesives

Have you ever watched a gecko walk up a glass window or hang upside down from the ceiling? It seems impossible, but geckos can stick to almost any surface without using any glue or sticky substances. How do they do it?

The secret is in their amazing toe pads. Each foot has about 500,000 tiny hairs, and each hair splits into even tinier branches. These are so small you'd need a powerful microscope to see them! When all these tiny hairs touch a wall or ceiling, they create an incredibly strong grip that lets geckos cling to almost anything, even glass!

It's like having millions of tiny magnets! Each tiny hair creates a small gripping force, but when millions of them work together, they add up to create incredibly strong holding power. The gecko can control this by changing the angle of its toes. When it wants to hold on, it presses them flat against the surface, and when it wants to let go, it peels them away.

Now here's where it gets exciting for us humans. Using this same system, scientists have developed gecko-inspired tapes and other materials that can stick to almost any surface, including underwater! These bio-inspired materials are reusable, don't leave residue, and work in extreme temperatures.

Doctors are excited about gecko-inspired bandages that hold perfectly but don't hurt when you remove them. They could also use gecko-style materials during operations when they need something to grip temporarily and then come off easily.

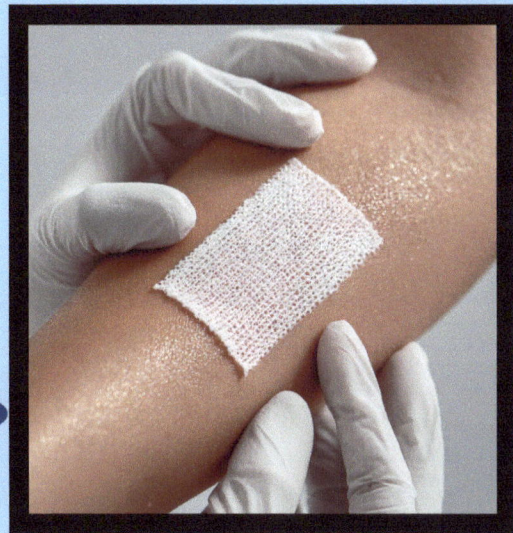

Rock climbers could use gecko-inspired gloves or shoes to climb any wall or cliff safely, and window washers on tall buildings could work without worrying about falling.

The gecko's amazing feet show us that nature's smallest features can hold the biggest secrets. Every time scientists study animals like geckos, they discover new ways to solve human problems.

The Sticky Secret of Velcro

In 1941, an engineer in Switzerland named Georges de Mestral was walking his dog through the countryside when he noticed how burr seeds stuck to both his clothes and his dog's fur. Instead of being frustrated like most people, he got curious. He examined the burrs under a microscope and discovered something amazing.

Each burr seed is covered with hundreds of small hooks. These microscopic hooks grab onto the loops in fabric fibers, animal fur, or anything with a similar texture. The hooks are so small and numerous that they create an incredibly strong connection that's also easy to pull apart when necessary.

This wasn't easy! It took Georges years of trying different materials to figure out how to make artificial hooks and loops that worked just like the burr seeds. Finally, he ended up creating two pieces. One piece was covered with small plastic hooks, like the burr seeds, and another piece covered with soft loops, like fabric. When you press the two pieces together, they form a strong bond that can be easily separated by pulling them apart.

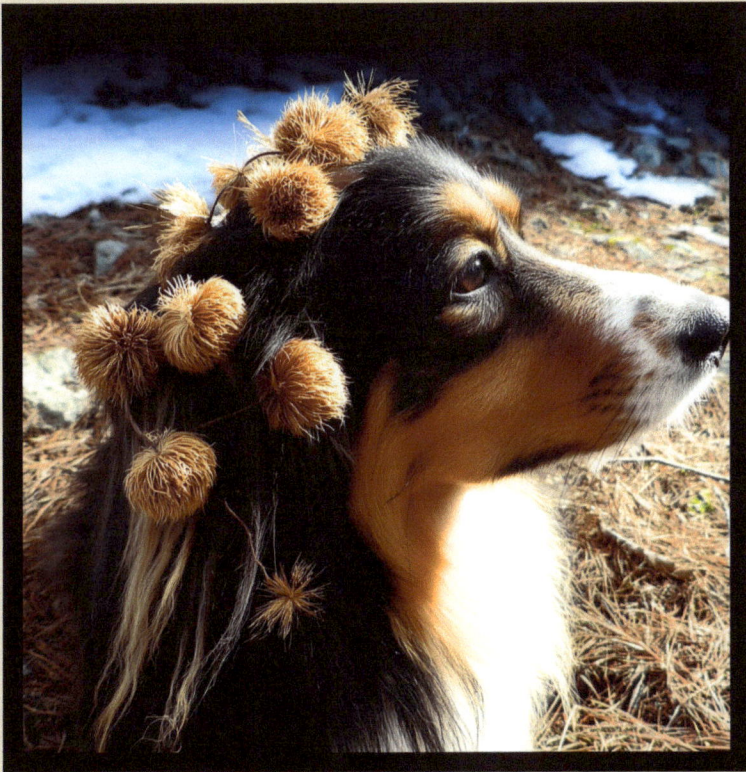

This is how Velcro was invented, and today, Velcro is everywhere! It's on shoes, backpacks, car seat covers, and baseball gloves. They even use Velcro in spaceships because it works perfectly in zero gravity, where other fasteners might float away.

This simple observation during a dog walk led to the creation of something that makes life easier for millions of people. Next time you hear Velcro's satisfying 'rip', remember, it all started with a curious engineer and some sticky seeds!

Shark Skin and Swimming Faster

Sharks are some of the ocean's best swimmers, and their skin plays a huge role in how fast they can swim and how easily they can move around in the water. If you could touch a shark's skin (which you definitely shouldn't try!), you'd be surprised to find it feels rough like sandpaper, not smooth like most fish.

But what makes shark skin so special? It is covered with tiny scales. These scales are not smooth like those on other fish. They're shaped like tiny teeth with ridges and points. When scientists looked closely at shark skin under powerful microscopes, they discovered that this rough texture helps water flow more smoothly over the shark's body, allowing sharks to swim faster while using less energy.

This discovery gave swimsuit designers a brilliant idea! They created swimsuits with fabric that mimicked these drag-reducing properties. Swimmers wearing these shark-skin-inspired suits broke so many world records that they were eventually banned from Olympic competition because they gave such an advantage!

But the innovations didn't stop there. Engineers have used these shark skin principles to design ships that travel through water more smoothly and use less fuel.

Airplane manufacturers are also experimenting with shark-skin-inspired surfaces to reduce airplane air resistance and improve fuel efficiency.

Scientists have also found that shark skin patterns can help reduce bacteria growth on hospital surfaces. The tiny ridges make it harder for germs to stick and multiply, which could help prevent infections.

Learning From Birds

For thousands of years, we have looked up at birds flying overhead and dreamt of one day being able to do the same. But it took us a long time to understand how birds fly and move so gracefully through the air.

Birds are incredible flying machines. Their wings aren't just simple flat surfaces. They're curved and can change shape while they fly! The curved shape of a bird's wing is the secret to flight. When a bird flaps its wings, air moves over its wings. The air moves faster over the curved top than under the flatter bottom. This creates a lifting force that pushes the bird up into the sky, just like when you blow air over the top of a piece of paper and it lifts up!

Our feathered friends can also change the shape of their wings to control their flight. They can twist their wings, adjust the angle, spread or fold their feathers, and even change the shape of individual feathers to steer, brake, or fly faster.

Early airplane designers like the Wright Brothers studied these amazing creatures carefully, especially how they controlled their flight by bending and twisting their wings. The Wright Brothers watched how birds could steer by changing the shape of their wings, and they copied this idea for their first successful airplane!

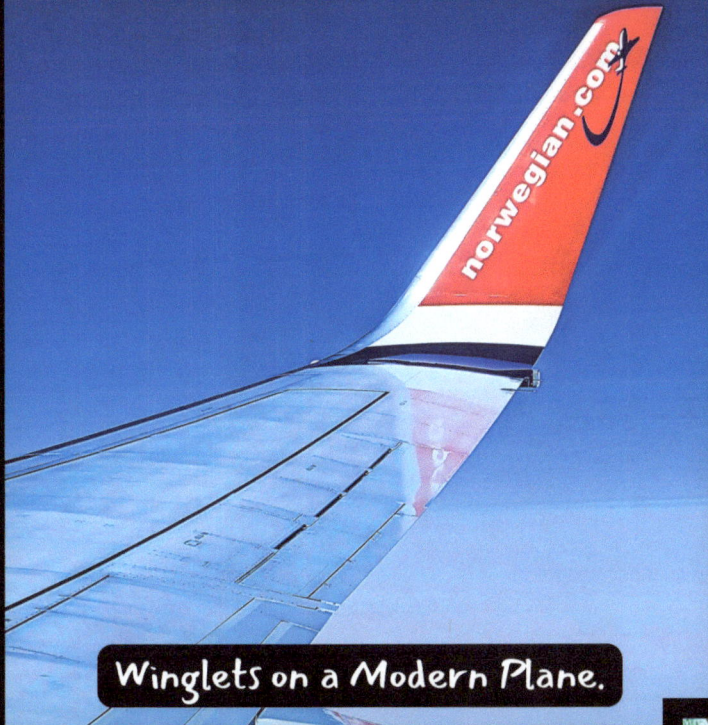

Winglets on a Modern Plane.

Modern airplanes still use ideas we learned from birds. The winglets you see on airplane wingtips, those curved parts that stick up, copy how birds spread their wing feathers to cut through the air more easily. Some new airplanes even have wings that can change shape during flight, just like bird wings!

Hummingbirds have inspired engineers to build tiny flying robots because hummingbirds can hover in one spot, fly backward, and zip around corners incredibly fast. These bird-inspired robots could help find people who are lost, check on wild animals in forests, or fly into dangerous places like burning buildings where it's too risky for people to go.

A Hummingbird.

Lotus Leaves And Self-Cleaning Surfaces

Have you ever seen a beautiful white lotus flower floating on a muddy pond? The leaves of lotus plants always look perfectly shiny, even though they live in murky, dirty water!

The secret is in the leaf's surface. Each lotus leaf is covered with thousands of tiny bumps, so small they would feel smooth to your fingers. But these invisible bumps are the key to the plant's cleaning superpower!

When raindrops or dew land on a lotus leaf, something magical happens. Instead of spreading out and getting the leaf wet, the water forms perfect little beads that roll around like tiny marbles. As these water beads roll across the leaf, they pick up any dirt, pollen, or dust on the surface and carry it away. The leaf stays completely clean and dry!

By studying the way lotus leaves clean themselves, scientists created special paints that shed rainwater and prevent dirt from sticking to building walls. Clothing companies that make jackets and pants for the outdoors also use this technology to create fabric that is easy to wash off mud and stains.

Window makers have developed coatings that let rain wash away bird droppings and dust without any scrubbing. Your smartphone or tablet screen might even use lotus-inspired coatings that make fingerprints and spills wipe away effortlessly!

From skyscrapers that stay spotless in the rain to hiking gear that cleans itself, the humble lotus leaf has revolutionized how we think about staying spotless. Sometimes nature's most elegant solutions are hiding right under our noses!

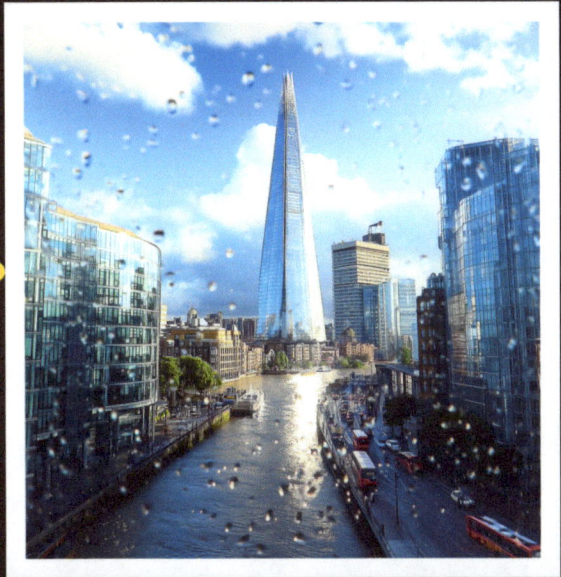

Rainwater pearling from the windows of a modern skyscraper.

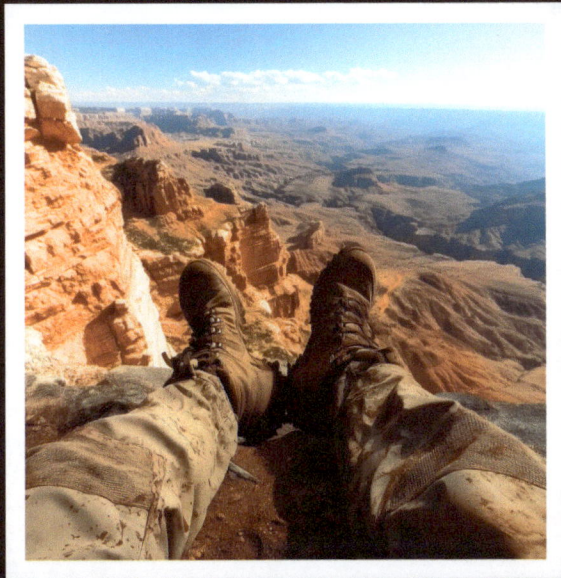

Clothing makers use fabric that is very easy to clean.

Smartphones use screens that stay smudge-free and clear.

Butterfly Wings and Brilliant Colors

Here's something cool about all the wonderful colors on a butterfly's wings. Their wings aren't actually colored at all! Instead of using colored materials like paint, butterfly wings are covered with tiny, clear structures that trick light into creating amazing colors.

You know how soap bubbles create beautiful rainbow colors? Butterfly wings work in a similar way. The wings are covered with thousands of tiny scales that have ridges so small you'd need a powerful microscope to see them. When the sun shines on these ridges, they reflect the light in special ways, creating brilliant blues, greens, and other colors.

This is why butterflies seem to change color when they move. The light hits their wings from different angles, so you see new shades and patterns! The best part? These colors never fade like paint because they're made from the shape of the wings, not colored materials.

Scientists studying butterfly wings have discovered how to use the same light-bending tricks to create computer and phone screens that can be seen perfectly even in bright sunlight. They also use much less battery power!

But that's not all. Engineers are also creating new kinds of paint and fabrics inspired by butterfly wings. These special paints create brilliant colors without harmful chemicals, and like butterfly wings, they never fade.

Kingfisher Beaks and Bullet Trains

The kingfisher is a bird that dives into water to catch fish. It can plunge into water at high speed and barely make a splash. Its long, pointed beaks are perfectly shaped to slice through water like a knife, allowing it to surprise its prey and catch its dinner.

In the 1990s, Japanese engineers worked on a super-fast train called a bullet train. When they started testing the train, called the Shinkansen, they realized that when the train zoomed out of tunnels, because it was traveling so fast, it created a thunderous noise that disturbed nearby communities.

One of the engineers, who loved watching birds, remembered how smoothly kingfishers entered the water. He wondered if the same idea could help trains move quietly through the air.

The team redesigned the front of the bullet train to look like the kingfisher's beak shape. The new sleek nose allowed the train to move through the air more efficiently, with less air pushing against it and eliminating the noise problem when exiting tunnels.

A Kingfisher Diving.

The results were incredible! The sharper nose allowed the train to cut through the air much more easily, making it even faster while using less energy. The redesign saved millions of dollars and made passenger train travel more comfortable.

This remarkable success story shows how observing nature can solve problems that seem totally unrelated to animals. A tiny bird's beak provided the perfect solution to an engineering challenge that had puzzled experts for years. Sometimes the best answers are flying right above our heads!

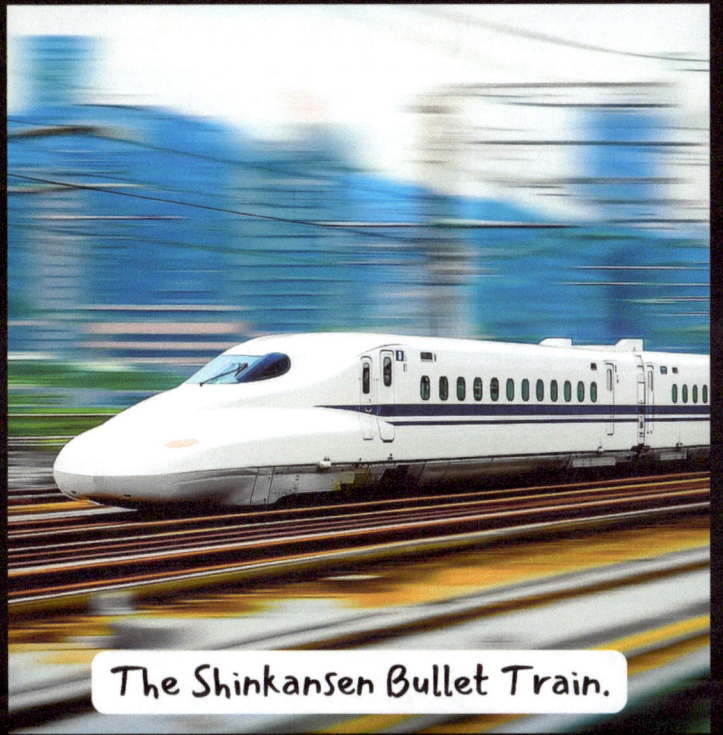

The Shinkansen Bullet Train.

Spider Silk and Super Materials

Spiders create one of the strongest materials on Earth using nothing but protein and water! The silk they create to make their webs is stronger than steel when you compare pieces of the same thickness. It can stretch better than rubber and is tougher than the material used to make bulletproof vests.

Most materials we have invented are strong but break easily, like glass, or flexible but weak, like rubber. Spider silk is incredibly strong and surprisingly bendy, making it very hard to break.

When we make super-strong materials like steel, we must heat them to incredibly high temperatures. When we want to make materials that bend easily, like rubber, we have to use very dangerous chemicals. Amazingly, spiders make their silk at normal temperatures using just water.

Here's the exciting part. Scientists have been trying for years to copy how spiders make silk. Some companies have even taught bacteria and other tiny creatures to make spider silk proteins, which can then be turned into thread.

The best part? Spider silk is completely natural and doesn't harm the environment. As we learn to make these materials like spiders, we could replace many artificial materials with ones that are better for our planet and work better too!

So, what could we do with spider-inspired materials? Imagine clothes lighter than cotton but stronger than armor, or fishing lines that dissolve safely in the ocean instead of polluting it. Doctors could also use spider silk thread for surgery that dissolves harmlessly in your body.

Termite Mounds and Natural Air Conditioning

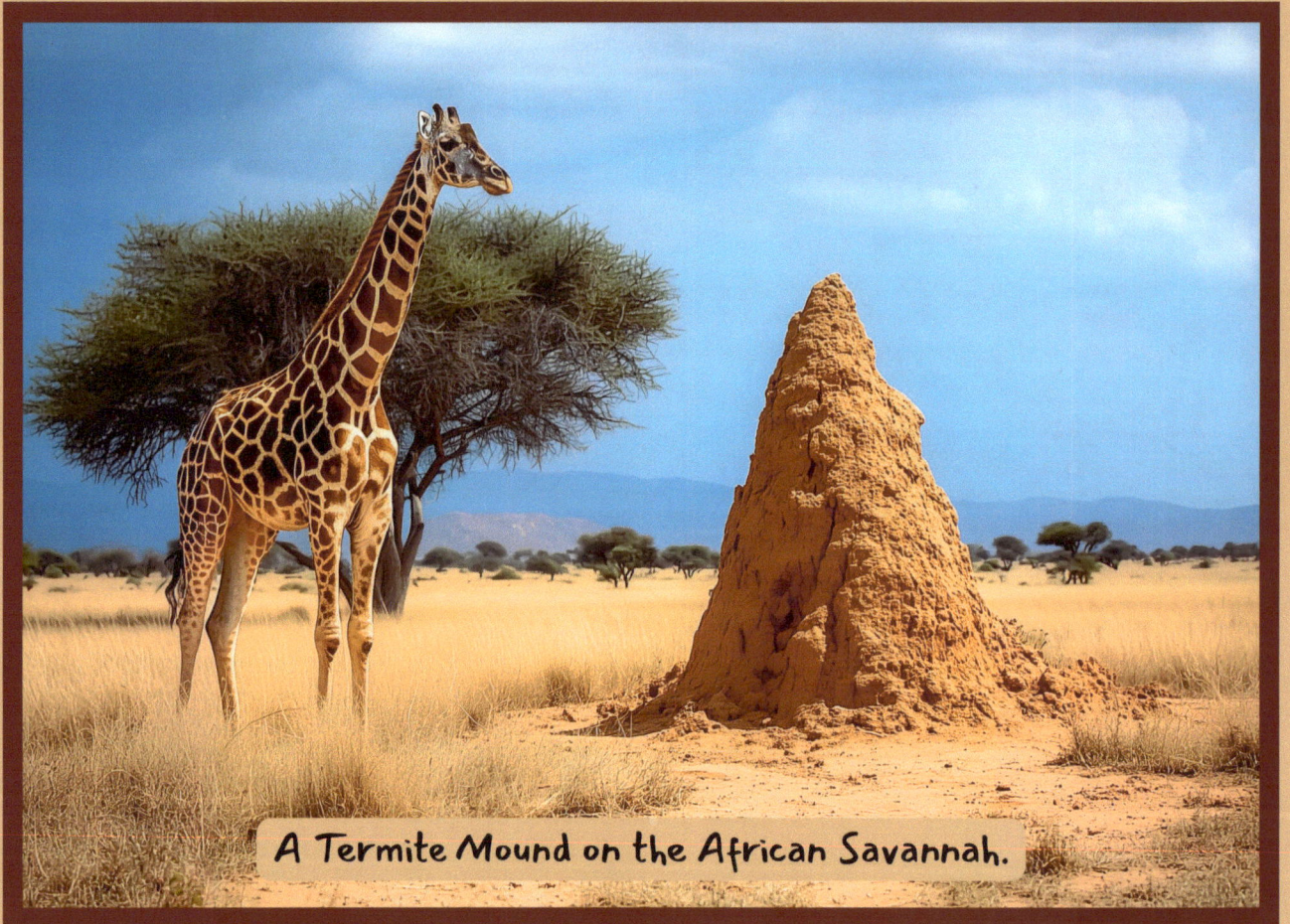

A Termite Mound on the African Savannah.

Tiny termites in Africa build some of Earth's most amazing air conditioning systems! These insects create towering mounds built impressively high, and they stay perfectly cool inside even when the desert sun makes the outside air scorching hot.

Here's how their incredible cooling system works. The termites build a maze of narrow tunnels and chimney-like vents throughout their mound. Cool air enters at the bottom, gets warmed up by all the busy termites living inside, then rises and flows through the top vents. This pulls fresh, cool air in from the bottom, creating a continuous breeze that keeps their home comfortable all day!

Scientists and architects were so impressed by this natural air conditioning that they decided to copy it for human buildings. The Eastgate Centre in Zimbabwe is a famous shopping mall that uses a termite-inspired design with large hollow columns and air shafts that work like termite tunnels.

During the day, warm air inside the building rises and flows out, pulling cooler air through the offices and shops. The system flips around at night, flushing out warm air so the building starts fresh and cool the next morning. This clever system uses a lot less energy than regular air-conditioning.

Scientists have even created special bricks with tiny air channels based on termite designs that brings down the costs of heating and cooling a building by a lot.

From tiny insects to massive shopping centers, termite engineering is helping us build smarter, greener buildings worldwide.

How Scientists Study Nature's Designs

Studying how animals and plants work is like being a detective, but instead of solving crimes, scientists are uncovering the coolest mysteries in the natural world!

The first step is watching very carefully. Scientists spend hours observing animals and plants, taking notes about how they move, eat, and survive. But here's where it gets really exciting. They use incredible tools that let them see things our eyes could never spot!

High-speed cameras can slow down a hummingbird's incredibly rapid wing beats to something we can watch step by step. Powerful microscopes show the tiny structures on a gecko's feet or the mini-scales on butterfly wings. Special sensors can even measure precisely how much force a mussel uses to stick to a rock underwater!

Once scientists understand how things in nature work, they face the challenge of copying these ideas using only human materials. This is where different types of scientists have to work together. Biologists understand how animals work, engineers design the new inventions, and materials experts figure out what to make them from.

Scientists also use computers to test their ideas. They create digital models of how shark skin moves through water or how bird wings create lift. Computer modelling helps them try out many different designs fast before they have to build anything real.

The coolest part is when scientists finally test their inventions in the real world. They might take their bird-inspired airplane wing to a wind tunnel, or test their shark-skin boat in a swimming pool. Sometimes their first try doesn't work perfectly, but that's okay! They go back to watching the animal again, looking for clues they might have missed.

Nature is full of amazing solutions waiting to be discovered. Every time scientists study a new animal or plant, they might find the next big invention that could change how we live, travel, or solve problems. Who knows? Maybe you'll be the next scientist to discover nature's next great secret!

Scientists use very powerful microscopes to study things too small for the human eye to see.

Engineers use wind tunnels to test and improve the design of airplanes.

Using computer modelling, engineers can test new designs before building them.

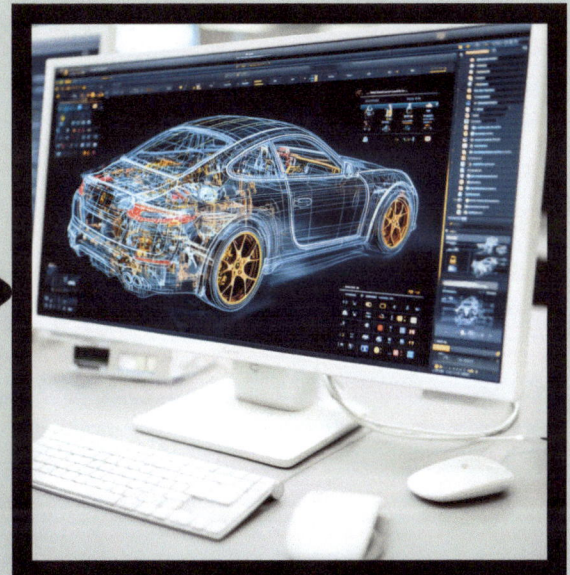

Protecting Nature

Nature is the world's biggest and best science lab, where amazing experiments have been running for millions of years! Every plant and animal has figured out incredible ways to survive, many of which are hiding secrets we haven't discovered yet.

This is why protecting all the different animals and plants on Earth is so important for biomimicry. When an animal or plant disappears forever, we lose all the amazing discoveries they might have taught us. Imagine if sharks had disappeared before we learned about their super-smooth skin, or if geckos had vanished before we figured out how their feet stick to walls!

Many of the coolest biomimicry discoveries happen when scientists study animals in their natural homes. They must see how animals live, hunt, and survive in the wild. When forests are cut down or oceans become polluted, we lose the chance to learn from these incredible creatures.

Climate change is making this problem even worse. As the world gets warmer, some animals might disappear before we can study them. Others might have to change how they live, and we could miss learning about their amazing abilities.

Here's some good news, though! When we copy nature's designs, we usually end up with better inventions for our planet. Nature doesn't create waste, doesn't use dangerous chemicals, and runs on energy from the sun. When we learn from nature, we can make cleaner, healthier choices, too.

You can help protect nature's amazing laboratory by supporting efforts to save endangered animals, learning about the creatures in your area, and making choices that help the environment. Every time we protect nature, we're saving the next great discovery!

Beeswax.

Honeybees build their hives using perfect hexagons (six-sided shapes) because this design uses the least amount of wax while storing the most honey. Now, engineers use the same hexagon pattern to make ultra-lightweight airplane parts!

Did you know?
Cat eyes reflect light so perfectly that road engineers copied them to create those reflective markers you see on highways that help drivers stay in their lanes at night!

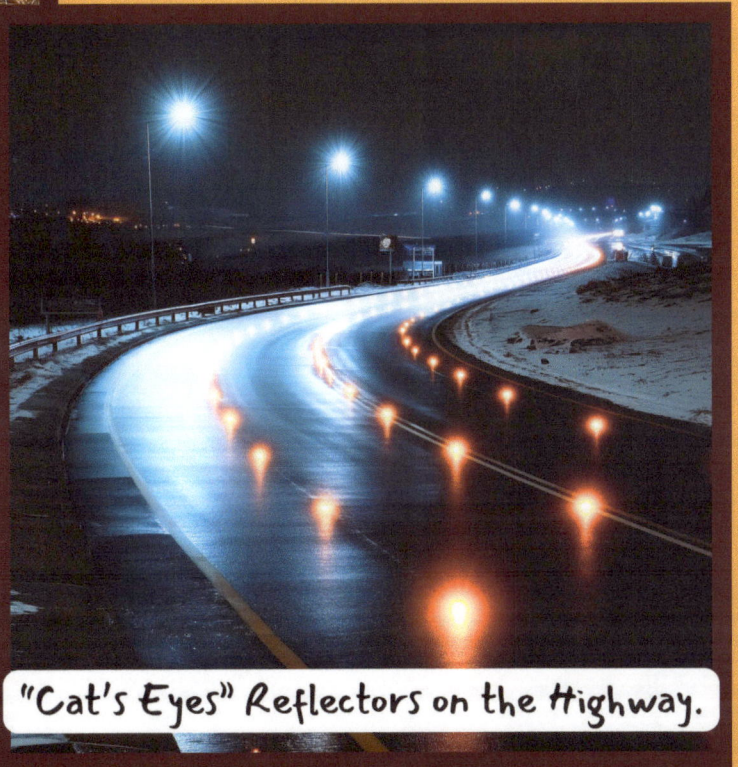

"Cat's Eyes" Reflectors on the Highway.

Young Inventors Who Inspire Us

Have you ever wondered if kids your age could discover something amazing that would change the world? Some of the most exciting inventions have come from young people who looked at nature with curious eyes and asked, "What if we could copy that?"

When Deepika Kurup was just 14, she saw children in India forced to drink dirty water. This bothered her so much that she decided to do something about it! She invented a solar-powered water cleaning system that uses sunlight to kill harmful germs in water. Her amazing invention earned her the title "America's Top Young Scientist" in 2012.

Thirteen-year-old Aidan Dwyer was hiking in the woods when he noticed something interesting about tree branches. They seemed to follow a spiral pattern! He discovered that trees arrange their branches according to a mathematical pattern called the Fibonacci sequence. Aidan wondered if solar panels arranged like tree branches might collect sunlight better than flat panels. When he tested his tree-inspired design, it worked! His spiral solar panels collected much more energy, especially during winter months.

These young inventors succeeded by combining careful observation of nature with creative thinking and hard work. They weren't afraid to ask questions and try new ideas, even when adults might have thought their ideas were unusual.

Careers in Biomimicry

If you love animals and plants and are curious about how nature solves problems, then biomimicry might be the perfect career for you! There are many exciting jobs for people who want to learn from nature and create amazing inventions. Here are just a few examples.

<u>Biomimicry Researchers</u> study animals and plants to discover how they do incredible things.

<u>Bioengineers</u> design and build new inventions inspired by animals and plants.

<u>Materials Scientists</u> try to make artificial versions of nature's super materials.

<u>Biomimicry Inventors</u> design and test new gadgets and tools inspired by nature in workshops and labs.

<u>Bio-inspired Architects</u> design buildings that work like living things!

<u>Robotics Engineers</u> watch how animals move and then build robots that can walk like dogs or swim like fish.

<u>Product Designers</u> create everyday items inspired by nature, from Velcro to better sports equipment.

<u>Biomimicry Teachers</u> help others learn about nature's amazing designs in schools, museums, and nature centers.

The future of biomimicry is incredibly exciting, and the tools we have available today make it easier than ever for young people to explore. You can use phone cameras to record nature, simple microscopes to examine tiny insects, and even 3D printers to test your bio-inspired designs.

Now that you know about biomimicry, you'll start seeing nature's incredible inventions everywhere! Every walk in the park becomes an opportunity for discovery.

We've learned how burr seeds inspired Velcro, how gecko feet led to amazing adhesives, how shark skin made swimmers faster, and how bird flight taught us to soar. But this is just the beginning! Scientists have explored only a small fraction of Earth's species, which means millions of natural innovations are still waiting to be discovered.

The key is to stay curious, observe the natural world carefully, and never stop asking questions. You don't need to become a scientist to contribute to biomimicry. Curiosity and creativity are what matter most.

So go outside, explore, and start your own biomimicry adventure. The next great nature-inspired invention might be waiting for you to be discovered!

Biomimicry Glossary

A _glossary_ is like a mini-dictionary of terms with definitions.

Here's a glossary of terms associated with _Biomimicry_.

Adhesive - A material that sticks things together, like glue or tape. Gecko feet inspired scientists to create new types of adhesives that can stick to almost any surface!

Aerodynamics - The study of how air moves around objects. Birds are masters of aerodynamics, which is why airplane designers study their wings.

Bacteria - Tiny living creatures so small you need a microscope to see them. Some bacteria can be taught to make spider silk proteins!

Bioluminescence - The ability of living things to create their own light, like fireflies, jellyfish, and some deep-sea fish. Scientists are studying this to create energy-efficient lighting.

Biomimetics - Another word for biomimicry. Both terms mean copying nature's designs to solve human problems.

Biomimicry - The science of copying nature's best ideas to solve human problems. "Bio" means life, and "mimicry" means to copy or imitate.

Bullet Train - A super-fast train that can travel over 200 miles per hour. The Japanese bullet train (Shinkansen) was redesigned to look like a kingfisher's beak to reduce noise and increase speed.

Camouflage - The way animals blend in with their surroundings to hide from predators or prey. Military uniforms and stealth technology are inspired by animal camouflage.

<u>Compound Eyes</u> - The type of eyes that insects have, made up of thousands of tiny lenses. These inspired new types of cameras and motion detectors.

<u>Drag</u> - The force that slows things down when they move through air or water. Shark skin helps reduce drag, which is why sharks are such fast swimmers.

<u>Echolocation</u> - The way animals like dolphins and bats "see" using sound waves. This natural ability inspired the invention of sonar and radar technology.

<u>Fibonacci Sequence</u> - A mathematical pattern found in nature where each number is the sum of the two before it (1, 1, 2, 3, 5, 8, 13...). Tree branches and leaves often follow this pattern, which inspired new solar panel designs.

<u>Gecko</u> - A small lizard that can walk on walls and ceilings. Geckos have millions of tiny hairs on their feet that create an incredibly strong grip without using any glue.

<u>Honeycomb</u> - The hexagonal (six-sided) pattern that bees use to build their hives. This shape is incredibly strong and inspired lightweight building materials and aircraft designs.

<u>Hydrophobic</u> - Materials that repel water, like a duck's feathers or lotus leaves. Scientists copy this property to create waterproof clothing and self-cleaning surfaces.

<u>Iridescence</u> - The way some animals like peacocks, beetles, and butterflies create shimmering, color-changing effects. This inspired new types of paints and displays that don't need pigments.

<u>Kevlar</u> - An extremely strong material used to make bulletproof vests. Spider silk is even tougher than Kevlar!

<u>Kingfisher</u> - A bird with a long, pointed beak that dives into water to catch fish. The kingfisher's beak shape inspired engineers to redesign bullet trains.

<u>Lift</u> - The upward force that allows birds and airplanes to fly. Understanding how bird wings create lift helped humans learn to fly.

<u>Lotus Effect</u> - The way lotus leaves stay perfectly clean by causing water to form beads that roll off, taking dirt with them. This natural cleaning trick inspired self-cleaning paints and fabrics.

<u>Magnetism</u> - Some animals like sea turtles and birds can sense Earth's magnetic field to navigate. Scientists are studying this to improve GPS and navigation systems.

<u>Microscopic</u> - So tiny that you need a microscope to see it clearly. Many of nature's amazing features, like the bumps on a beetle's shell or the hooks on burr seeds, are microscopic.

<u>Mussel</u> - A type of shellfish that creates incredibly strong underwater glue to stick to rocks. This inspired new medical adhesives that work inside the human body.

<u>Nanocoating</u> - An extremely thin layer of material applied to surfaces to give them special properties, like making smartphone screens fingerprint-resistant. Inspired by butterfly wings and lotus leaves.

<u>Photosynthesis</u> - The way plants use sunlight to make food and energy. Solar panels are inspired by how leaves capture and use sunlight.

<u>Protein</u> - A natural material that living things use to build parts of their bodies. Spiders make their incredibly strong silk using only protein and water.

<u>Self-cleaning</u> - Surfaces that clean themselves without scrubbing or soap. Lotus leaves are naturally self-cleaning, which inspired scientists to create similar materials for buildings and clothes.

<u>Self-healing</u> - Materials that can repair themselves when damaged, just like how our skin heals cuts. Scientists are developing self-healing concrete and plastics inspired by biological healing.

<u>Shinkansen</u> - The Japanese name for their bullet train system. Engineers redesigned the train's nose to look like a kingfisher's beak after noise problems.

<u>Sonar</u> - A system that uses sound waves to detect objects underwater, inspired by how dolphins and whales navigate. Submarines and ships use sonar technology.

<u>Spider Silk</u> - The strong, flexible material spiders use to make their webs. It's stronger than steel, stretchier than rubber, and made at room temperature using just protein and water.

<u>Streamlined</u> - Having a smooth, pointed shape that moves easily through air or water. Fish, birds, and sharks all have streamlined bodies that inspired vehicle designs.

Surface Tension - The force that allows some insects to walk on water. Understanding this helped scientists create new materials and tiny robots.

Termite Mound - The tall towers that termites build to live in. These mounds have amazing natural air conditioning systems that keep them cool inside even in hot desert climates.

Van der Waals Forces - The tiny attractive forces between molecules that help geckos stick to surfaces. These forces are so small that millions are needed to create a strong grip.

Velcro - A fastener made of tiny hooks and loops that stick together. It was invented after studying how burr seeds stick to clothing and animal fur.

Ventilation - The movement of fresh air through a space. Termite mounds and prairie dog burrows have natural ventilation systems that inspired building designs.

Wind Tunnel - A special room where scientists test how air flows around objects like airplane wings. They use wind tunnels to test bio-inspired designs before building real aircraft.

Winglets - The curved tips you see on airplane wings that stick up or down. They copy how birds spread their wing feathers to fly more efficiently and use less fuel.

Biomimicry Quiz

Multiple Choice Questions (Choose the best answer)

1. What does the word "biomimicry" mean?
   a) Studying animals in zoos
   b) Copying nature's designs to solve human problems
   c) Taking pictures of plants and animals
   d) Building robots that look like animals

2. Where do Andy and Lila visit that has the world's oldest desert?
   a) Egypt
   b) Australia
   c) Namibia
   d) Chile

3. How many tiny hairs does each gecko foot have?
   a) About 50,000
   b) About 500,000
   c) About 5,000,000
   d) About 50

4. What year did Georges de Mestral invent Velcro?
   a) 1941
   b) 1951
   c) 1961
   d) 1971

5. What does shark skin feel like when you touch it?
   a) Smooth like glass
   b) Slimy like a fish
   c) Rough like sandpaper
   d) Soft like fur

6. What creates lift that allows birds to fly?
   a) Air moving faster under the wing than over it
   b) Air moving faster over the wing than under it
   c) Birds flapping their wings really hard
   d) The bird's tail feathers

7. Why do lotus leaves always look clean?
   a) They grow in clean water
   b) Water beads up and rolls off, taking dirt with it
   c) They have a waxy coating
   d) Fish clean them

8. How do butterfly wings create colors without using pigments?
   a) They use tiny mirrors
   b) They absorb certain colors of light
   c) Tiny structures reflect light in special ways
   d) They change temperature

9. What bird inspired the redesign of Japanese bullet trains?
   a) Eagle
   b) Hummingbird
   c) Kingfisher
   d) Owl

10. What is spider silk stronger than when comparing pieces of the same thickness?
    a) Rope
    b) Steel
    c) Plastic
    d) Wood

11. How do termites keep their mounds cool in hot desert climates?
    a) They live underground
    b) They use a natural air conditioning system with tunnels and vents
    c) They only come out at night
    d) They cover their mounds with mud

12. What tool can slow down a hummingbird's wing beats so scientists can study them?
    a) Telescope
    b) High-speed camera
    c) X-ray machine
    d) Stethoscope

13. What percentage of Earth's species have scientists studied for biomimicry?
    a) About 50%
    b) About 25%
    c) Less than 10%
    d) About 75%

14. How old was Deepika Kurup when she invented her water cleaning system?
    a) 12
    b) 14
    c) 16
    d) 18

15. What mathematical pattern did Aidan Dwyer notice in tree branches?
    a) Fibonacci sequence
    b) Prime numbers
    c) Perfect squares
    d) Multiplication tables

16. The Namib Desert beetle collects water from:
    a) Underground springs
    b) Morning fog
    c) Rainwater
    d) Nearby rivers

17. Which building in Zimbabwe uses termite-inspired cooling design?
    a) Eastgate Centre
    b) Victoria Centre
    c) Harare Mall
    d) Desert Tower

18. What happens to swimmers wearing shark-skin inspired suits in the Olympics?
    a) They swim slower
    b) They were eventually banned because they gave too much advantage
    c) They get disqualified
    d) Nothing special

19. Scientists studying how dolphins navigate inspired which technology?
    a) GPS
    b) Sonar
    c) Radar
    d) Telescopes

20. What do engineers call the curved tips on airplane wings that copy bird feathers?
    a) Winglets
    b) Featherlets
    c) Air tips
    d) Flight strips

Fill-in-the-Blank Questions

21. The word "bio" means _____ and "mimicry" means to copy or imitate.

22. The Namib Desert is more than _____ million years old.

23. Gecko feet work like having millions of tiny _____ that create a strong grip.

24. Georges de Mestral got the idea for Velcro while walking his _____ and noticing burr seeds.

25. Shark skin has tiny scales shaped like _____ with ridges and points.

26. The Wright Brothers studied how birds _____ and _____ their wings to control flight.

27. When water lands on a lotus leaf, it forms perfect little _____ that roll around like tiny marbles.

28. Butterfly wings are covered with thousands of tiny _____ that have ridges.

29. The Japanese bullet train is also called the _____.

30. Spiders make silk using only _____ and water at normal temperatures.

31. Termite mounds have _____ and chimney-like _____ that create airflow.

32. Scientists use _____ cameras to study how hummingbirds fly.

33. When forests are cut down, we lose the chance to learn from _____ creatures.

34. A _____ Researcher studies animals and plants to figure out how they do incredible things.

35. Deepika Kurup won the title "America's Top Young _____" in 2012.

36. The tiny bumps on a Namib Desert beetle's shell are smaller than the width of _____ on your head.

37. Special sensors can measure how much _____ a mussel uses to stick to rocks underwater.

38. The lotus effect helps create self-_____ materials for buildings and clothing.

39. Engineers test their bio-inspired airplane designs in _____ tunnels.

40. Nature doesn't create _____ and runs on energy from the sun.

True/False Questions

41. Biomimicry always creates inventions that look exactly like the animals or plants they copy.

42. Gecko feet use sticky glue to stick to surfaces.

43. Velcro works perfectly in zero gravity, which is why it's used in spaceships.

44. All fish have smooth skin like most people think sharks do.

45. Birds can change the shape of individual feathers to control their flight.

46. Lotus leaves stay clean because they grow in clean water.

47. Butterfly wings actually contain colored pigments like paint.

48. The kingfisher-inspired bullet train design made trains slower but quieter.

49. Spider silk is tougher than the material used to make bulletproof vests.

50. Termites are too small to build effective air conditioning systems.

51. Scientists have studied most of Earth's species for biomimicry applications.

52. Young people have never made important biomimicry discoveries.

53. High-speed cameras can slow down motion so fast that scientists can study hummingbird wing beats.

54. Climate change could cause us to lose animals before we can study their amazing abilities.

55. You need to become a scientist to contribute to biomimicry discoveries.

56. The Namib Desert beetle's water collection system works by channeling water directly into its mouth.

57. Lotus-inspired coatings on smartphone screens help repel fingerprints and spills.

58. The Eastgate Centre in Zimbabwe uses 85% less energy than buildings with regular air conditioning.

59. Spider silk can only be made at extremely high temperatures like steel.

60. Gecko-inspired adhesives leave sticky residue when removed.

61. Butterfly wing colors fade over time just like regular paint.

62. Shark skin patterns can help reduce bacteria growth on hospital surfaces.

63. Burr seeds stick to fabric because they have a natural glue coating.

64. Modern airplanes still use ideas learned from studying bird flight.

65. The kingfisher's beak inspired engineers because it makes a loud noise when entering water.

66. Hummingbird-inspired robots could be used for search and rescue operations.

67. Andy and Lila's dad is a doctor who told them about biomimicry.

68. Biomimicry inventions are usually worse for the environment than traditional technologies.

69. Scientists use computer models to test their bio-inspired designs before building real prototypes.

70. Aidan Dwyer was 17 years old when he made his solar panel discovery.

Quiz Answer Key

Multiple Choice	Fill-in-the-Blank	True/False	
1. b	21. life	41. False	61. False
2. c	22. 55	42. False	62. True
3. b	23. magnets	43. True	63. False
4. a	24. dog	44. False	64. True
5. c	25. teeth	45. True	65. False
6. b	26. bend, twist	46. False	66. True
7. b	27. beads	47. False	67. False
8. c	28. scales	48. False	68. False
9. c	29. Shinkansen	49. True	69. True
10. b	30. protein	50. False	70. False
11. b	31. tunnels, vents	51. False	
12. b	32. high-speed	52. False	
13. c	33. incredible	53. True	
14. b	34. Biomimicry	54. True	
15. a	35. Scientist	55. False	
16. b	36. hair	56. True	
17. a	37. force	57. True	
18. b	38. cleaning	58. True	
19. b	39. wind	59. False	
20. a	40. waste	60. False	

Hands-on Activities You Can Try At Home

Now that you've learned about nature's amazing designs, here are some safe, fun ways to explore biomimicry yourself!

The Velcro Investigation: Ask an adult to help you collect some burr seeds. Examine them with a magnifying glass. Look at how the tiny hooks grab onto different materials like fabric, fur, or yarn. Try gently pressing velcro strips together and pulling them apart while listening to the sound. Can you hear individual hooks releasing?

Bird Flight Observations: Spend time watching birds in your area. Maybe you can borrow Grandpa's binoculars or use your eyes. Do you notice how different birds fly differently? How do birds land on branches? Draw pictures of different wing shapes and flight patterns you observe. You can even try making paper airplanes with different wing shapes inspired by the birds you've watched.

Water Drop Olympics: Fill a spray bottle with water and test how water behaves on different surfaces. Use leaves, feathers, plastic, fabric, and wax paper. Which surfaces make water bead up and roll off? Which ones absorb water? This experiment helps you understand how some animals stay dry and how others collect water.

Seed Helicopter Challenge: Collect maple seeds (the "helicopters" that spin as they fall) and drop them from different heights. Ask an adult to help you time with a stopwatch how long it takes to fall and observe their spinning motion. Try making your own paper helicopters and see if you can design one that falls as slowly as the real seeds.

Nature's Shapes Hunt: Look for patterns and shapes that repeat in nature. These can be like the spirals in shells and pinecones, hexagons in honeycomb, or the branching patterns in trees and rivers. Sketch these patterns and think about why these shapes appear in nature so often.

Always remember to observe nature safely and respectfully. Never disturb animals or damage plants, and always have an adult help you with any outdoor activities.

Take a look at other subjects Lila and Andy are learning about...

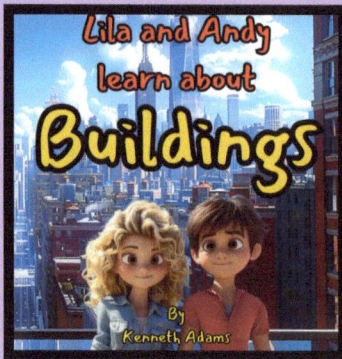
Lila and Andy learn about Buildings
By Kenneth Adams

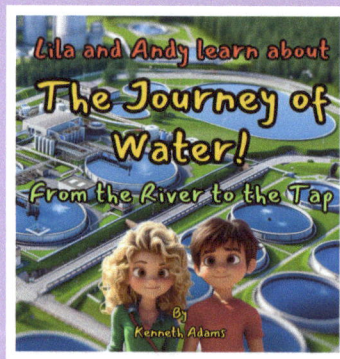
Lila and Andy learn about The Journey of Water!
From the River to the Tap

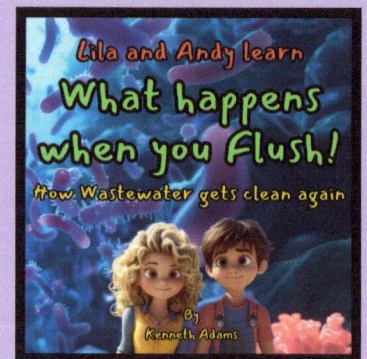
Lila and Andy learn What happens when you Flush!
How Wastewater gets clean again
By Kenneth Adams

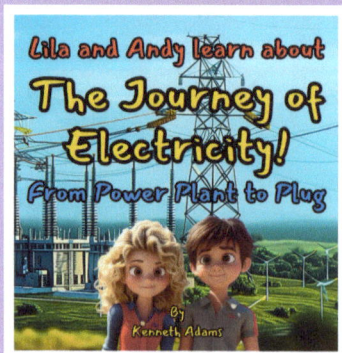
Lila and Andy learn about The Journey of Electricity!
From Power Plant to Plug
By Kenneth Adams

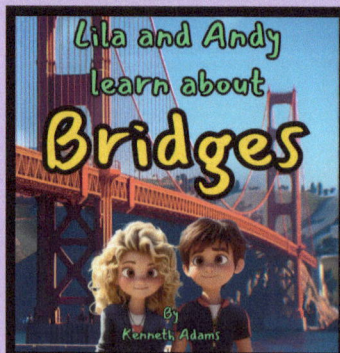
Lila and Andy learn about Bridges
By Kenneth Adams

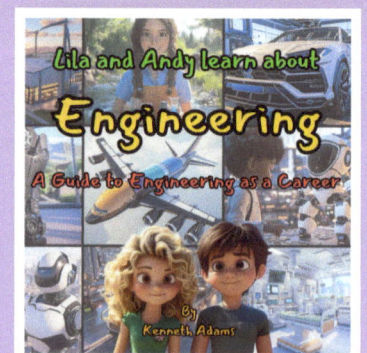
Lila and Andy learn about Engineering
A Guide to Engineering as a Career
By Kenneth Adams

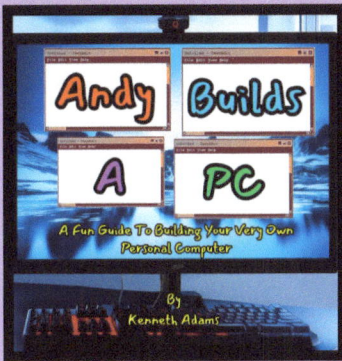

Andy Builds A PC
A Fun Guide To Building Your Very Own Personal Computer
By Kenneth Adams

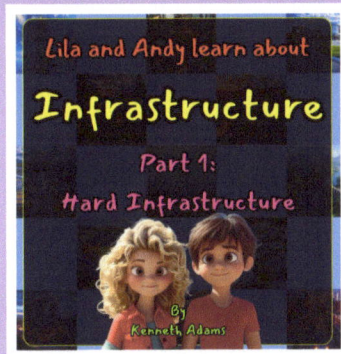

Lila and Andy learn about
Infrastructure
Part 1:
Hard Infrastructure
By Kenneth Adams

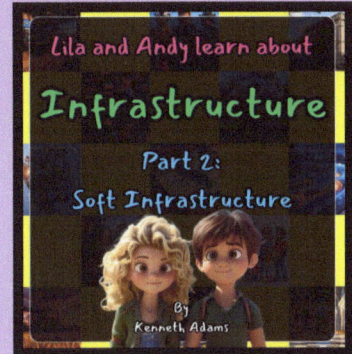

Lila and Andy learn about
Infrastructure
Part 2:
Soft Infrastructure
By Kenneth Adams

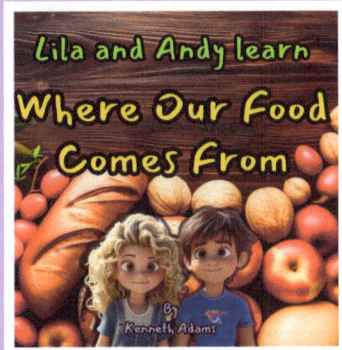

Lila and Andy learn
Where Our Food Comes From
By Kenneth Adams

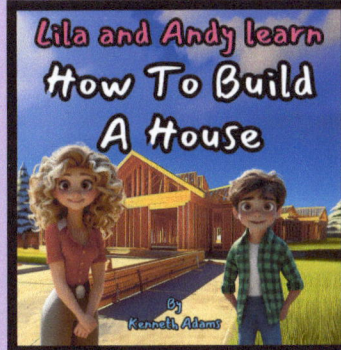

Lila and Andy learn
How To Build A House
By Kenneth Adams

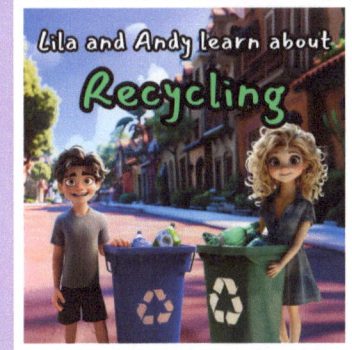

Lila and Andy learn about
Recycling

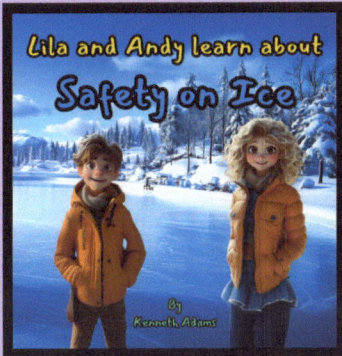

Lila and Andy learn about
Safety on Ice
By Kenneth Adams

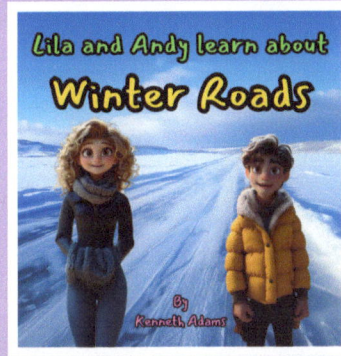

Lila and Andy learn about
Winter Roads
By Kenneth Adams

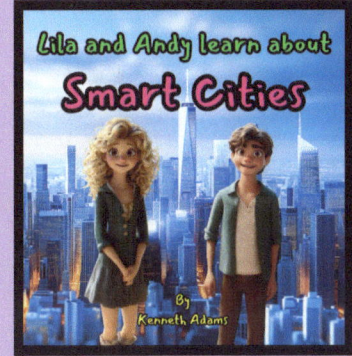

Lila and Andy learn about
Smart Cities
By Kenneth Adams

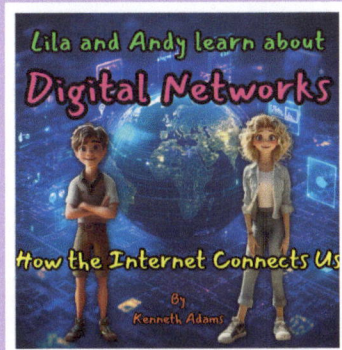

Lila and Andy learn about
Digital Networks
How the Internet Connects Us
By Kenneth Adams

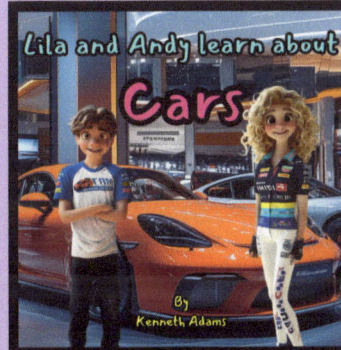

Lila and Andy learn about
Cars
By Kenneth Adams

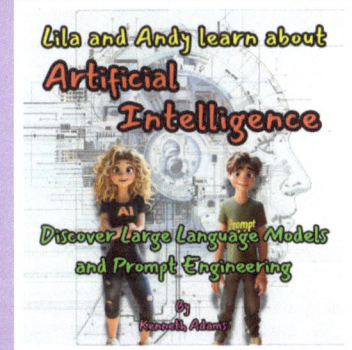

Lila and Andy learn about
Artificial Intelligence
Discover Large Language Models and Prompt Engineering
By Kenneth Adams

www.ingramcontent.com/pod-product-compliance
Lightning Source LLC
Chambersburg PA
CBHW042013080426
42734CB00003B/66